W9-BPQ-353

INFORMATION
EXPLORER
JUNIOR

Designing a Winning Science Fair Project

by Sandy Buczynski

CHERRY LAKE PUBLISHING · ANN ARBOR, MICHIGAN

A NOTE TO PARENTS AND TEACHERS: Please remind your children how to stay safe online before they do the activities in this book.

CHERRY LAKE
Publishing

A NOTE TO KIDS: Always remember your safety comes first!

Published in the United States of America
by Cherry Lake Publishing
Ann Arbor, Michigan
www.cherrylakepublishing.com

Content Adviser: Gail Dickinson, PhD, Associate
Professor, Old Dominion University, Norfolk, Virginia

Photo Credits: Cover, ©iStockphoto.com/Jbryson; page 5, ©IrinaK/Shutterstock.com;
page 11, ©Sergey Novikov/Shutterstock.com; page 16, ©Raywoo/Shutterstock.com;
page 19, ©karelnoppe/Shutterstock.com.

Library of Congress Cataloging-in-Publication Data
Buczynski, Sandy, author.
  Designing a winning science fair project / by Sandra Buczynski.
    pages cm. — (Information explorer junior)
  Audience: K to grade 3. Includes bibliographical references and index.
  ISBN 978-1-63137-790-7 (lib. bdg.) — ISBN 978-1-63137-810-2 (pbk.) —
ISBN 978-1-63137-850-8 (e-book) — ISBN 978-1-63137-830-0 (pdf)
  1. Science projects—Juvenile literature. I. Title.

  Q182.3.B83 2015
  507.8—dc23   2014002774

Cherry Lake Publishing would like to acknowledge the work of The Partnership for
21st Century Skills. Please visit *www.p21.org* for more information.

Printed in the United States of America
Corporate Graphics Inc.
July 2014

Table of Contents

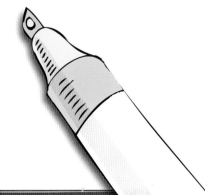

CHAPTER ONE

What Is a Science Project?

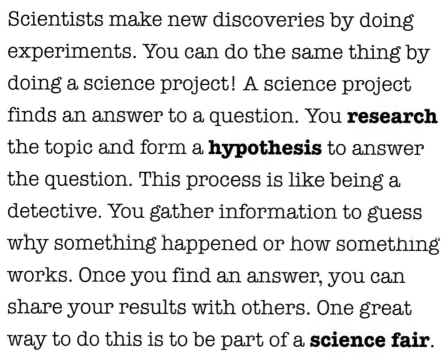

Scientists make new discoveries by doing experiments. You can do the same thing by doing a science project! A science project finds an answer to a question. You **research** the topic and form a **hypothesis** to answer the question. This process is like being a detective. You gather information to guess why something happened or how something works. Once you find an answer, you can share your results with others. One great way to do this is to be part of a **science fair**.

The key to a good science fair project is curiosity. When you are curious, you ask a lot of questions. You see something and wonder what causes it. You notice something and wonder why it happens. You want to know how something works. What do you wonder about? What puzzles you?

A science fair project is usually an experiment. It can also be an invention. You can invent something to fix a problem. You can invent something that improves on an older invention, too. For example, you could

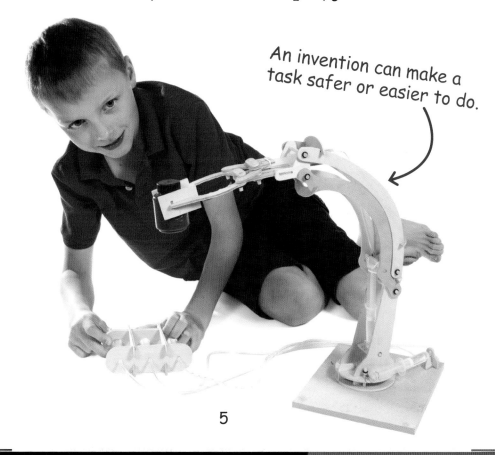

An invention can make a task safer or easier to do.

invent a new way to recycle old things. Or you could invent a faster way to make fruit turn ripe. Science projects can also be models that show something. For example, you could show how a magnet works.

Neil's teacher asked him to do a project for his school's science fair. Neil looks around him for ideas for a topic. He thinks about his interests, checks the Internet, and reads stories. He finds an idea he likes in "Goldilocks and the Three Bears." In this story, Goldilocks tastes three bowls of porridge (porridge is like oatmeal). One bowl of porridge is too hot. One is too cold. The last one is just right. How could this be? Neil decides to do a science project to figure it out!

Why did the bowls of porridge have different temperatures?

To get a copy of this activity, visit www.cherrylakepublishing.com/activities.

Try This

BRAINSTORM

Think of a topic that really interests you. If you are having trouble, go to the Science Buddies Web site (*www.sciencebuddies.org*).

Do you have a topic ready? Let's brainstorm a question that can be tested with a science project. Try making a mind map. Use Neil's mind map below as an example. Draw a circle and write your main question in the center. Then make bubbles for possible answers to your main question. Draw lines to connect them to your center circle. You can use these questions to decide what your project will be.

What if the bowls were different sizes?

What if each bowl held a different amount of porridge?

How can the three bowls of porridge be different temperatures?

What if the bowls were made from different things, such as wood or plastic?

What if one bowl was covered and the others were not?

CHAPTER TWO

Gathering Information

Neil must learn more about his topic. One way he can do this is by using his senses. He can look, listen, touch, smell, or maybe even taste to get more information about his topic. Another way he can learn more is to ask questions of his teachers, librarians, or parents. Finally, Neil can read books and articles or browse the Internet for more information.

Neil takes notes about the things he learns. Scientists keep detailed notes about everything they learn in a science notebook. Neil keeps a science notebook, too. He also includes a list of the books and Web sites he uses.

Next, it is time to form a hypothesis. A good hypothesis is based on the information you gather. Neil uses his notes and observations to decide what he thinks will happen. A prediction can be put into this sentence:

If I change _____, then I predict____ (will happen).

Neil thinks about why the bowls of porridge were different temperatures. His guess goes into the first blank. What will he be measuring? This answer goes into the second blank.

If I change the size of the bowl, then I predict the temperature will be highest in the biggest bowl.

Form a hypothesis based on the thing you will be changing.

If I change the amount of porridge in each bowl, then I predict the temperature will be highest in the bowl with the most porridge.

To get a copy of this activity, visit
www.cherrylakepublishing.com/activities.

Try This

Record Your Information

Go to the library or use the Internet to start gathering information about your topic. Use the following form to keep track of the sources you are using.

Type of source: —————————
(*book, Web site, magazine, etc.*)

Author of source: —————————
(*last name, first name*)

Title of source: —————————

Web site address (if needed): —————————

Record this information for each of the sources you use.

CHAPTER THREE

Experimenting

An experiment will help you find out if your hypothesis is true or not.

Now it is time for Neil to test his hypothesis. He does this by conducting an experiment. It is important for an experiment to be a fair test. This means Neil must change only one thing at a time. Everything else in the experiment is kept the same. This allows Neil to figure out what is causing his results.

Things that change in an experiment are called **variables**. A good experiment has only one variable that is changed on purpose. Another variable is counted, measured, or observed. Neil uses his hypothesis sentence to identify these two variables. All of the other variables in the experiment are kept the same.

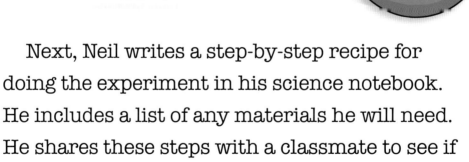

Variable that is changed on purpose

If I change the size of the bowl, then I predict the temperature will be highest in the biggest bowl.

Variable that is measured

PAPA BEAR

Next, Neil writes a step-by-step recipe for doing the experiment in his science notebook. He includes a list of any materials he will need. He shares these steps with a classmate to see if that person can follow his directions.

Changed Variable		
Big Bowl		
Medium Bowl		
Small Bowl		

What will Neil be counting or measuring in his experiment? This will be his data. Data are the results from an experiment. Neil makes a **data table** so that he can quickly write down the measurements from the experiment.

Now Neil carries out his experiment. He follows the steps he wrote down. He measures carefully. He uses words, drawings, and photos to tell what is happening. Then he does it all again! Scientists always double-check their results. Each time Neil does the same experiment is called a **trial**. Neil's results should be the same for each trial. If they are not, he must find what changed in each trial. He makes sure only one variable changed each time. He adjusts his experiment until he gets the same results over and over again.

Try This

Let's make a fair test for finding out why three bowls of porridge might be different temperatures.

1. Gather your materials.
   - 3 packages of instant oatmeal
   - 3 thermometers
   - A thermos of hot water
   - Three bowls—one small, one medium, and one large—made of the same material (wood, plastic, or glass)
2. Make a data table. Put the variable that is being changed along the left side of the chart. Put the variable that is being measured across the top. The units of measurement are the times (starting time and after 10 minutes) and the related temperatures (in degrees Fahrenheit and Celsius).

Changed Variable	Starting Temp. °C (°F)	After 10 minutes Temp. °C (°F)
Big Bowl		
Medium Bowl		
Small Bowl		

3. Follow the steps of the fair test.

   a. Put one package of oatmeal in each different-size bowl. The size of the bowl is the variable you change.

   b. Add exactly one cup of hot water from the thermos to each bowl and stir.

   c. Take the temperature of the oatmeal in each bowl. This is the variable you are measuring. Record your data.

   d. Wait 10 minutes and take another temperature reading for each bowl. Record your data.

CHAPTER FOUR

Explaining Your Results

The notes from your experiment will help you find an answer to the question you asked.

What does it all mean? Once Neil has his data, he explains his results. Graphs and pictures can make data easier to understand. Neil organizes his data into a graph.

To get a copy of this activity, visit www.cherrylakepublishing.com/activities.

Try This

Here is an example of possible data Neil might get from the porridge experiment:

Changed Variable	Starting Temp. °C (°F)	After 10 minutes Temp. °C (°F)
Big Bowl	77°C (170°F)	55°C (131°F)
Medium Bowl	77°C (170°F)	65°C (149°F)
Small Bowl	77°C (170°F)	75°C (167°F)

Let's use this data to make a bar graph. Each bar represents one of the three bowls. The graph allows us to see the results clearly and form a **conclusion**. A conclusion answers the question, "What have I learned from my experiment?" You can divide your conclusion into three sections.

1. *Decide if an experiment's results match the hypothesis.* Neil's hypothesis was that the temperature would be highest in the biggest bowl.

Continued on page 18. →

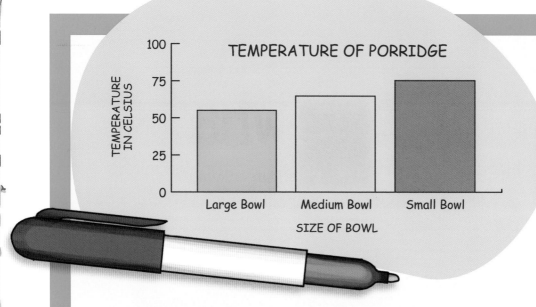

The results show that the biggest bowl had the lowest temperature. Neil's hypothesis was not true. That is OK. Even an incorrect hypothesis gives useful information.

2. *Answer the question asked at the beginning of the project.* Neil asked, "How can the bowls of porridge be different temperatures?" Neil's data shows that the bowls were different sizes.

3. *Mention things that went wrong.* Was something spilled after being measured? Did Neil write down a number wrong? These and other mistakes can affect the results of an experiment.

4. *Do the experiment again for a second trial.*

CHAPTER FIVE

Sharing What You Learned

There are many ways to share your results.
Be creative!

Scientists want to share their work with
others. Neil shares his experiment at a
science fair. So can you! A science fair is a

fun time when everyone gets together and shows off the results from their science projects. Parents and friends are invited to walk around and look at the projects. There might even be judges who look at all the different projects and pick a winner.

Include the following when sharing your project:

- What was your question?
- What was your hypothesis?
- What experiment did you do and what were the results?
- What's the answer to your question? Was your hypothesis true or false?
- What other experiments could you do using the new things you learned?

A three-panel board is a great way to present your experiment. A simple display is best. Neatness counts! The title should be catchy and describe your project.

Question/Purpose
State the problem you meant to solve.

Hypothesis
State your hypothesis.

Procedures
Explain the experiment. What? How? Why?

PROJECT TITLE
by Your Name

Data and Graphics
Display your data and photos in this area. Graphics are very effective for explaining results.

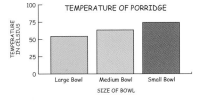

TEMPERATURE OF PORRIDGE

TEMPERATURE IN CELSIUS

100
75
50
25
0

Large Bowl   Medium Bowl   Small Bowl

SIZE OF BOWL

Results
What did you learn from your work? Explain you data.

Conclusion
Was your hypothesis right or wrong? Can you make a new one?

Recommendations
From what you learned, would you try anything new?

A three-panel poster is a great way to share your findings!

A science project gives you a chance to think like a scientist. Each experiment you do answers a question. The answers will lead to even more questions. Stay curious!

Glossary

conclusion **(kuhn-KLOO-zhuhn)** a final decision, thought, or opinion

data table **(DAY-tuh TAY-buhl)** a chart that organizes the information collected during an experiment into columns and rows

hypothesis **(hy-POTH-uh-sihss)** a logical guess about what will happen in an experiment

research **(REE-surch)** to collect information about a subject through reading, investigating, or experimenting

science fair **(SYE-uhns FAYR)** an event where students gather to show the results of their science project to judges and visitors

trial **(TRYE-uhl)** the act of trying or testing something

variables **(VAIR-ee-uh-buhlz)** things that can change during an experiment

Find Out More

BOOKS

Buczynski, Sandra. *Get Ready for a Winning Science Project.* Ann Arbor, MI: Cherry Lake Publishing, 2012.

Margles, Samantha. *Star Wars: Science Fair Book.* New York: Scholastic, 2013.

WEB SITES

Education.com—Second Grade Science Fair Project Ideas

www.education.com/science-fair/second-grade

Check out some examples of science projects you can do at home.

Science Buddies

www.sciencebuddies.org

Gather information and get ideas for new science projects.

Index

About the Author

Sandy Buczynski, PhD, is an associate professor in math, science, and technology education at the University of San Diego in California. Big *mahalos* go out to Donna, Mary, Michele, Cheryl, and Bobbi for their wonderful science project input!